INTRODUCTION

Almost everyone enjoys a sweet finale to dinner or an occasional sweet treat for a snack. To satisfy a sweet tooth, look to this collection of enticing recipes featuring high quality confection products from Kraft – caramels, marshmallows and marshmallow creme.

This book features desserts from simple Mallow Fruit Dip to more sophisticated show-stoppers like Brownie-Mint Alaska and Praline Souffle. It offers recipes for freshly baked pies such as Caramel Pecan and simple, no-bake creations like Luscious Freeze Pie. There are quick and easy snack recipes – Marshmallow Crispy Treats and Caramel Corn. America's passion for chocolate is sweetly satisfied with recipes for Fantasy Fudge, Decadent Brownies and Chocolate Caramel Pecan Cheesecake.

It was in the 1930s, when Kraft was busy using its knowledge of dairy technology to improve the quality of butterscotch, that it discovered a new product – caramels. Kraft caramels by the bag were first sold in 1938 and were an immediate success both as a candy and as a cooking ingredient.

Kraft's next achievement was to develop a revolutionary new marshmallow which was soft and fluffy, unlike its traditional "crusty" predecessor. From consumer mail, Kraft knew cooks liked to add marshmallows to salads, sweet potatoes and desserts, but cutting the marshmallows into small pieces was a tedious and sticky job. Recipe-size marshmallows (miniature marshmallows) was the successful solution. Kraft also extended its line of marshmallow products in 1959 with the introduction of marshmallow creme, which was smooth and fluffy, and blended easily with other ingredients.

Throughout the years, Kraft has continued to offer good food ideas and imaginative recipes using their versatile confection products. Today, many cooks are interested in easy-to-make, time-saving, no-fail recipes. Kraft caramels, marshmallows and marshmallow creme fit well with these contemporary cooking trends. For those interested in gourmet, up-scale cooking and entertaining, Kraft confections fill that need, too.

With pride and pleasure, Kraft presents this fine collection of recipes which is sure to provide many sweet moments in your culinary future.

ANGEL FLAKE, BAKER'S, COOL WHIP, FUNMALLOWS, GERMAN'S, JELL-O, JET-PUFFED, KRAFT, KRAFT Hexagon Logo, MINUTE, PARKAY, PHILADELPHIA BRAND and ZAP AN APPLE are trademarks of Kraft General Foods, Inc., Glenview, IL 60025.

CLB 2599
© 1992 Colour Library Books Ltd., Godalming, Surrey, England.
All rights reserved
This edition published in 1992 by
SMITHMARK Publishers, Inc., 112 Madison Avenue, New York, N.Y. 10016
Printed and bound in Singapore.
ISBN 0 8317 3194 X

SMITHMARK books are available for bulk sales promotion and premium use. For details write or telephone the Manager of Special Sales, SMITHMARK Publishers Inc., 112 Madison Avenue, New York, NY 10016. (212) 532-6600.

MARSHMALLOW CRISPY TREATS

Makes 2 dozen

This all-time kids' favorite makes a big hit in lunch boxes and at scout meetings. A microwave oven makes this easy recipe even easier.

¼ cup PARKAY Margarine
1(10½oz) bag (6 cups) KRAFT Miniature
    Marshmallows
6 cups crisp rice cereal

1. Melt margarine in 3-quart saucepan over low heat. Add marshmallows, stirring until melted and well blended. Remove from heat. Alternatively, microwave margarine in large mixing bowl on HIGH 45 seconds or until melted. Add marshmallows; toss to coat with margarine. Microwave 1½ minutes or until smooth when stirred, stirring after 45 seconds.

2. Stir in cereal until well coated; then press into a greased 13 x 9-inch baking pan.

STEP 2

3. Cool and cut into squares.

STEP 1

STEP 3

Cook's Notes

🕐 TIME: Preparation takes 10 minutes. Cooking takes 10 minutes.

❓ VARIATIONS: Substitute a 10oz bag KRAFT JET-PUFFED Marshmallows or a 10½ oz bag FUNMALLOWS Miniature Marshmallows for Miniature Marshmallows.
    You can also substitute one 7oz jar KRAFT Marshmallow Creme for marshmallows – melt margarine in 3-quart saucepan over low heat. Add marshmallow creme, mixing until well blended. Continue cooking, stirring constantly, for 5 minutes over low heat. Continue as directed.

👨‍🍳 COOK'S TIP: Use a piece of lightly greased wax paper to press the hot cereal mixture into the pan.

TEXAS TRUFFLES

Makes about 38-40

Cooking is fun with this new version of a popular confection. Marshmallows are dipped in chocolate then rolled in toasted coconut, nuts or sprinkles.

1 (10oz) bag KRAFT JET-PUFFED Marshmallows
1 (12oz) package BAKER'S Semi-Sweet Real
　　Chocolate Chips
BAKER'S ANGEL FLAKE Coconut, toasted
Chopped pecans
Multi-colored sprinkles

STEP 3

1. Arrange marshmallows on tray and freeze for 15 minutes.

2. Microwave chocolate chips in glass bowl on HIGH for 1 minute. Stir; microwave for 1 minute. Stir and microwave a further 30 seconds or until smooth.

4. Roll chocolate-coated marshmallows in coconut, chopped nuts or sprinkles.

STEP 2

STEP 4

3. Using a skewer or fondue fork, dip marshmallow into melted chocolate until marshmallow is chocolate coated.

5. Use another fork or metal spatula to place marshmallow onto wax paper lined tray.

6. Chill or keep in cool dry place.

Cook's Notes

🕐 TIME: Preparation takes 20 minutes. Microwave cooking takes 2½ minutes.

🍴 COOK'S TIP: If chocolate cools and becomes too thick while dipping, simply return it to the microwave for a few additional seconds.

FANTASY FUDGE

Makes 3 pounds

This creamy, smooth fudge has been one of Kraft's "most requested" recipes for years. Placed in a decorative tin, this fudge is a welcomed hostess gift during the holidays.

¾ cup PARKAY Margarine
3 cups sugar
⅔ cup evaporated milk
1 (12oz) package BAKER'S Semi-Sweet Real
　　Chocolate Chips
1 (7oz) jar KRAFT Marshmallow Creme
1 cup chopped nuts
1 tsp vanilla

---

1. Microwave margarine in 4-quart bowl or casserole on HIGH 1 minute or until melted. Add sugar and milk; mix well. Microwave on HIGH 5 minutes or until mixture begins to boil; stir after 3 minutes. Mix well, scrape bowl. Microwave 5½ minutes, stirring after 3 minutes.

STEP 1

Alternatively, stir together margarine, sugar and milk in heavy 2½ to 3-quart saucepan; bring to full boil, stirring constantly. Boil 5 minutes over medium heat, or until candy thermometer reaches 234°, stirring constantly to prevent scorching. Remove from heat.

2. Gradually stir in chocolate chips until melted. Add remaining ingredients, mixing until well blended.

STEP 2

3. Pour into greased 9 x 9-inch or 13 x 9-inch pan. Cool at room temperature and cut into squares.

STEP 3

Cook's Notes

🕐 TIME: Preparation takes 10 minutes, cooking takes 15 minutes.

🔧 COOK'S TIPS: At high altitude decrease recommended temperature (234°) 2 degrees for every 1,000 feet above sea level. For successful fudge, be sure to use evaporated milk, not sweetened condensed milk.

❓ VARIATIONS: Substitute 1 cup peanut butter for chocolate chips. Substitute 4 cups KRAFT Miniature Marshmallows for KRAFT Marshmallow Creme. Substitute 1 cup KRAFT Party Mints or Butter Mints for nuts. Substitute 1 cup KRAFT Peanut Brittle, crushed for nuts. Substitute ½ cup crushed peppermint candy for nuts.

FIVE-CUP SALAD

Serves 4-6

Just five ingredients and one measuring cup are needed for this refreshing salad. What could be simpler?

1 cup orange sections
1 cup KRAFT Miniature Marshmallows
1 cup sour cream
1 cup grapes
1 cup BAKER'S ANGEL FLAKE Coconut

1. To segment an orange, use a serrated fruit knife to peel the zest, starting at the top of the orange and working around to the bottom.

STEP 2

3. In large bowl, mix together all ingredients. Chill.

STEP 3

STEP 1

2. Cut each segment away by slicing between membranes with the knife.

Cook's Notes

🕐 TIME: Preparation takes 10 minutes plus chilling.

❓ VARIATIONS: Substitute 1 cup peach slices or one 11oz can mandarin orange segments (drained), for the orange sections. Add one (8oz) can pineapple chunks, drained.

⬭ SERVING IDEA: Five-Cup Salad is a tasty accompaniment to ham or roast chicken.

FUDGEMALLOW CANDY

Makes about 2 dozen squares

With only three ingredients, this peanut butter-chocolate confection is a snap to make.

1 (12oz) package BAKER'S Semi-Sweet Real
   Chocolate Chips
1 cup chunk style peanut butter
1 (6¼oz) bag (3½ cups) KRAFT Miniature
   Marshmallows

1. Melt chocolate chips with peanut butter in saucepan over low heat, stirring until smooth. Alternatively, microwave chocolate chips and peanut butter in 2-quart bowl on MEDIUM (50%) 2-3 minutes or until melted, stirring after each minute.

STEP 1

2. Fold in marshmallows.

STEP 2

3. Pour into greased 9-inch square pan and chill until firm. Cut into squares.

STEP 3

Cook's Notes

🕐 TIME: Preparation takes 5 minutes. Cooking takes 5 minutes plus chilling.

❓ VARIATION: Fold in ½ cup raisins with marshmallows.

🍞 COOK'S TIP: Fudgemallow Candy keeps best in the refrigerator.

CHOCO MALLOW PIZZA
Serves 10-12

This pizza is unlike any you've ever tasted! It's really a delicious chocolate, marshmallow, rice cereal and peanut concoction garnished to resemble a pizza with red and green maraschino cherries. Try it on your favorite teen.

---

1 (12oz) package BAKER'S Semi-Sweet Real
    Chocolate Chips
1 lb white almond bark, divided
2 cups KRAFT Miniature Marshmallows
1 cup crisp rice cereal
1 cup peanuts
1 (6oz) jar red maraschino cherries, drained and
    cut in half
3 tbsps green maraschino cherries, drained and
    quartered
⅓ cup BAKER'S ANGEL FLAKE Coconut
1 tsp oil

---

1. In large saucepan, melt chocolate chips with 14 ounces of the almond bark over low heat, stirring until smooth. Remove from heat.

STEP 1

2. Stir in marshmallows, cereal and peanuts. Pour onto greased 12-inch pizza pan. Top with cherries and sprinkle with coconut.

STEP 2

3. Melt remaining almond bark with oil over low heat, stirring until smooth; drizzle over coconut. Chill until firm and store at room temperature.

STEP 3

Cook's Notes

🕐 TIME: Preparation takes 15 minutes plus chilling.

❓ VARIATION: Substitute 1 cup chopped or halved pecans or walnuts for peanuts.

◣ PREPARATION: Smaller-size pizzas make nice gifts. Shape mixture into four 6-inch rounds or twelve 4-inch rounds on wax paper-lined cookie sheets.

CATHEDRAL WINDOW HOLIDAY BARS

Makes about 3 dozen

For a truly festive cookie tray, try these tasty bars. When the bars are cut, the colorful marshmallows mixed with the rich chocolate may remind you of beautiful stained glass windows.

Crust
¾ cup PARKAY Margarine
¾ cup powdered sugar
1½ cups flour

Filling
2 (4oz) packages BAKER'S GERMAN'S Sweet
  Chocolate
¾ cup PARKAY Margarine
¼ cup half and half
2 cups powdered sugar
1 (10½oz) bag FUNMALLOWS Miniature
  Marshmallows
1 cup chopped pecans

1. Preheat oven to 350°F.

2. In small mixing bowl, beat margarine and sugar on electric mixer until light and fluffy. Add flour; mix well. Press onto bottom of 13 x 9-inch baking pan.

STEP 2

3. Bake 12-15 minutes or until golden brown; cool.

4. Melt chocolate with margarine over low heat, stirring constantly, until smooth.

STEP 4

5. Beat chocolate mixture, half and half and powdered sugar until well blended. Fold in marshmallows and pecans; spread over crust. Chill. Cut into bars.

STEP 5

Cook's Notes

⏱ TIME: Preparation takes 25 minutes plus chilling.

🖥 COOK'S TIP: To melt chocolate and margarine in the microwave, break chocolate into squares and microwave with margarine in small bowl on HIGH 1½-2 minutes or until almost melted, stirring after 1 minute. Stir until smooth.

GRASSHOPPER TORTE
Serves 10-12

The heavenly flavor combination of chocolate and mint is featured in this frozen dessert.

Crust
2 cups (24) crushed, cream-filled chocolate
    cookies
¼ cup PARKAY Margarine, melted

Filling
1 (7oz) jar KRAFT Marshmallow Creme
¼ cup creme de menthe
2 cups whipping cream, whipped

1. To make the crust, combine crumbs and margarine. Reserve ½ cup for topping and press remaining crumb mixture onto bottom of 9-inch springform pan.

STEP 1

2. For the filling, combine the marshmallow creme and creme de menthe, mixing with electric mixer or wire whisk until well blended.

STEP 2

3. Fold in whipped cream. Pour over crust.

STEP 3

4. Sprinkle with remaining crumbs. Freeze.

Cook's Notes

⏱ TIME: Preparation takes 15 minutes plus freezing.

❓ VARIATIONS: Substitute ¼ cup milk for creme de menthe, and stir in a few drops of peppermint extract and food coloring. Substitute 2 cups chocolate wafer crumbs for cream-filled chocolate cookies.

👨‍🍳 COOK'S TIP: When a dinner menu calls for lots of last minute preparation, plan a dessert such as Grasshopper Torte, that can be made well in advance. Freeze the dessert uncovered until firm, then wrap tightly for storage.

MALLOW FRUIT DIP

Makes about 1½ cups

Your guests will enjoy this creamy orange dip with luscious fresh fruit dippers, especially on hot summer days.

1 (8oz) package PHILADELPHIA BRAND Cream Cheese, softened
1 (7oz) jar KRAFT Marshmallow Creme
1 tbsp orange juice
1 tsp grated orange peel
Dash of ground ginger (optional)

STEP 1

1. In small mixing bowl, beat ingredients with an electric mixer until well blended.

2. Serve with fruit.

STEP 1

STEP 2

Cook's Notes

⏱ TIME: Preparation takes 10 minutes.

❓ VARIATION: Substitute 1 tbsp lime juice and 1 tsp grated lime peel for orange juice and peel.

◻ SERVING IDEA: Serve this dip with fresh fruit such as strawberries, melon balls, pineapple chunks, apple or nectarine slices, bananas or grapes.

👨‍🍳 COOK'S TIP: To soften cream cheese, microwave in bowl on MEDIUM (50%) for 30 seconds. To easily remove Marshmallow Creme from jar, remove lid and seal and microwave on HIGH 30 seconds.

MALLOW-WHIPT SWEET POTATOES

Serves 6

These fluffy sweet potatoes are enhanced with orange juice and cinnamon and topped with lightly-browned miniature marshmallows. Your kids will forget they're eating vegetables.

STEP 2

2 (17oz) cans sweet potatoes, drained and mashed
2 cups KRAFT Miniature Marshmallows
¼ cup PARKAY Margarine, melted
¼ cup orange juice
½ tsp cinnamon

1. Preheat oven to 350°F.

2. In large bowl, stir together sweet potatoes, 1 cup marshmallows, margarine, juice and cinnamon. Spoon into 1-quart casserole.

3. Bake in preheated oven 20 minutes. Sprinkle with remaining marshmallows and broil until lightly browned.

STEP 2

STEP 3

Cook's Notes

⏱ TIME: Preparation takes 15 minutes. Cooking takes 20 minutes.

❓ VARIATION: Recipe may be doubled. Spoon into 2-quart casserole. Continue as directed.

⭘ SERVING IDEA: These sweet potatoes are the perfect accompaniment to turkey, ham or roast pork.

👨‍🍳 COOK'S TIP: Sweet potatoes are an excellent source of Vitamin A.

ROCKY ROAD BROWNIES

Makes about 2 dozen

It's easy to jazz up a packaged brownie mix with just a sprinkle of marshmallows and nuts and a drizzle of melted chocolate. Delicious!

1 (20-23oz) package brownie mix
2 cups KRAFT Miniature Marshmallows
1 cup BAKER'S Semi-Sweet Real Chocolate Chips, melted
¼ cup milk
½ cup coarsely chopped nuts

1. Prepare brownie mix and bake as directed on package for cake-type brownies.

2. Immediately sprinkle marshmallows over brownies; continue baking until marshmallows begin to melt.

3. Melt chips with milk over low heat, stirring until smooth. Drizzle over marshmallows and sprinkle with nuts.

STEP 3

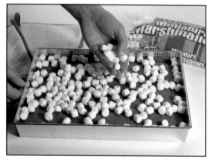

STEP 2

STEP 3

4. Cool and cut into bars.

Cook's Notes

TIME: Preparation takes 5 minutes. Cooking takes 30 minutes.

COOK'S TIP: Store brownies, covered, at room temperature.

MARSHMALLOW WALDORF SALAD

Serves 4-6

This classic apple salad is made extra special with marshmallows and grapes.

3 cups chopped red apple
1 cup celery slices
1 cup grape halves
1 cup KRAFT Miniature Marshmallows
¼ cup chopped walnuts
KRAFT Real Mayonnaise

2. Halve the grapes.

STEP 2

1. Chop the apple and slice the celery.

STEP 1

3. Mix apples, marshmallows, celery, grapes, walnuts and mayonnaise to moisten. Chill.

STEP 3

Cook's Notes

TIME: Preparation takes 15 minutes plus chilling.

COOK'S TIP: Choose firm, crisp "eating" apples for salads. Varieties such as Delicious, Jonathan and McIntosh are popular.

STRAWBERRY ICE

Serves 6-8

Relax with this light, refreshing berry ice on warm summer evenings. It's a delicious way to top off most any meal.

4 cups strawberry halves
1 (7oz) jar KRAFT Marshmallow Creme
1 tbsp lemon juice
1 tsp grated lemon peel

1. Place strawberries in blender container or food processor work bowl. Cover; process until smooth.

STEP 1

2. Gradually add strawberries to marshmallow creme in large bowl of electric mixer, mixing until well blended. Blend in juice and peel.

STEP 2

3. Pour into 9-inch square pan and freeze until almost firm.

4. Coarsely chop mixture. Spoon into chilled bowl and beat with electric mixer until smooth, then freeze.

STEP 4

Cook's Notes

🕐 TIME: Preparation takes 15 minutes plus freezing.

👨‍🍳 COOK'S TIP: The trick to blending liquid ingredients with marshmallow creme is to add the liquid ingredients very gradually in the beginning.

🅾 SERVING IDEA: Serve garnished with extra strawberries and strawberry leaves.

BROWNIE-MINT ALASKA

Serves 8-10

Looking for a magnificent show-stopping dessert? Look no further than Brownie-Mint Alaska and be assured, no one will guess how easy it was to make.

1 qt. mint ice cream, softened
1 (13-16oz) package brownie mix
3 egg whites
1 (7oz) jar KRAFT Marshmallow Creme

1. Press ice cream into 1-quart mixing bowl lined with foil and freeze.

STEP 1

2. Prepare mix as directed on package for cake-type brownies. Bake in greased 8-inch layer pan. Cool 10 minutes and then remove from pan. Set aside to cool further.

3. Preheat oven to 450°F.

4. Beat egg whites until soft peaks form. Gradually add marshmallow creme, beating until stiff peaks form.

STEP 4

5. Place brownie on lightly greased cookie sheet. Unmold ice cream onto brownie and remove foil. Completely cover ice cream and brownie with meringue.

STEP 5

6. Bake 3-4 minutes or until lightly browned.

Cook's Notes

⏱ TIME: Preparation takes 15 minutes plus freezing. Cooking takes 35 minutes.

◆ PREPARATION: Separate egg whites from yolks while eggs are at refrigerator temperature, being careful not to break the yolks. Let egg whites stand until they are room temperature to obtain the greatest volume when beating.

👨‍🍳 COOK'S TIP: Work quickly when spreading the meringue so the ice cream does not begin to melt. To make a decorative design with the meringue, gently press the back of a spoon into the meringue in a swirling motion and lift up for peaks.

CALIFORNIA WHITE CHOCOLATE FUDGE

Makes about 2½ pounds

"Truly elegant" just begins to describe this creamy, white chocolate confection that is studded with crunchy walnuts and golden dried apricots. It makes a wonderful hostess gift!

1½ cups sugar
¾ cup sour cream
½ cup PARKAY Margarine
12 oz white chocolate, coarsely chopped
1 (7oz) jar KRAFT Marshmallow Creme
¾ cup chopped walnuts
¾ cup chopped dried apricots

1. In heavy 2½ to 3-quart saucepan, bring sugar, sour cream and margarine to full, rolling boil over medium heat, stirring constantly. Continue boiling 7 minutes or until candy thermometer reaches 234°F, stirring constantly.

2. Remove from heat and stir in chocolate until melted.

STEP 2

3. Stir in remaining ingredients until well blended. Pour into greased 8 or 9-inch square baking pan. Cool several hours or overnight. Cut into squares before serving.

STEP 1

STEP 3

Cook's Notes

⏱ TIME: Preparation takes 30 minutes plus chilling.

👨‍🍳 COOK'S TIPS: To easily remove marshmallow creme from jar, remove lid and

seal and microwave on HIGH 30 seconds. Use good quality white chocolate, such as that found in candy stores.

❓ VARIATION: Substitute macadamia nuts for walnuts.

ZAP AN APPLE™

Caramel Apples

Serves 4-5

You'll be amazed how quickly caramels melt when you "zap" them in the microwave.

4 – 5 medium size apples
Wooden sticks
1 (14oz) bag KRAFT Caramels
2 tbsps water

1. Wash and dry apples; insert stick into stem end of each apple.

STEP 2

3. Dip apples into hot caramel sauce, turning until coated. Scrape excess sauce from bottom of apples.

STEP 1

2. Microwave caramels and water in small deep glass bowl on HIGH 2½ to 3½ minutes, stirring after each minute until sauce is smooth. (If caramel sauce is too thin, let stand about 2 minutes before dipping apples.) Alternatively, melt caramels with water in 1½-quart heavy saucepan over low heat, stirring frequently until smooth.

STEP 3

4. Place on greased wax paper. Store in refrigerator. Let stand at room temperature 15 minutes before serving to allow caramel to soften.

Cook's Notes

⏰ TIME: Preparation takes 20 minutes plus chilling.

❓ VARIATIONS: Substitute pears for apples. Add 2 tbsps creamy peanut butter with caramels and water and roll in chopped peanuts. Dip caramel-coated apples in flaked coconut, chocolate chips or KRAFT Miniature Marshmallows, cut in half.

CHOCOLATE CARAMEL NUT BARS

Makes 2 dozen

Start with a cake mix for these sinfully delicious, irresistible bars. The recipe makes enough for sharing at your next potluck or picnic.

---

1 (14oz) bag KRAFT Caramels
1 (5 fl oz) can evaporated milk, divided
1 two-layer German chocolate cake mix with
    pudding
½ cup PARKAY Margarine, melted
1 cup BAKER'S Semi-Sweet Real Chocolate Chips
1½ cups chopped walnuts, divided

---

1. Preheat oven to 350°F.

2. In medium saucepan, melt caramels with ⅓ cup milk over low heat, stirring until smooth. Set aside.

STEP 3

4. Sprinkle chocolate chips and 1 cup walnuts over crust; top with caramel mixture and spread to edges of pan. Top with teaspoonfuls of remaining cake mixture; press gently into caramel mixture. Sprinkle with remaining walnuts.

STEP 2

3. In a large bowl, mix together remaining milk, cake mix and margarine. Press half of cake mixture onto bottom of ungreased 13 x 9-inch baking pan. Bake 8 minutes.

STEP 4

5. Bake 16-18 minutes. Cool and cut into bars.

Cook's Notes

TIME: Preparation takes 25 minutes. Cooking takes 18 minutes.

COOK'S TIP: Microwave caramels with milk in 2-quart bowl on HIGH 3-4 minutes or until sauce is smooth, stirring every 2 minutes.

? VARIATIONS: Substitute chocolate cake mix for German chocolate cake mix. Substitute pecans for walnuts.

CARAMEL CORN

Makes 2½ quarts

There is nothing like homemade caramel corn with the rich buttery flavor of quality caramels. Make a batch for Halloween this year.

28 KRAFT Caramels
2 tbsps water
2½ qts. popped corn

1. Microwave caramels and water in medium bowl on HIGH 1½ minutes; stir. Continue microwaving 30 seconds to 1 minute or until sauce is smooth, stirring every 30 seconds. Alternatively, melt caramels with water in heavy saucepan over low heat, stirring until smooth.

2. Pour over popped corn and toss until well coated. Spread onto greased cookie sheet to form single layer.

STEP 2

3. Let stand until set, then break apart.

STEP 1

STEP 3

Cook's Notes

TIME: Preparation takes about 20 minutes.

VARIATIONS: Decrease popped corn to 2 qts. and add ½ cup peanuts.

COOK'S TIP: For crispier caramel corn, prepare popcorn mixture as directed. Spread onto greased cookie sheet and bake at 250°F for 25 minutes. Break apart before serving.

CREAMY CARAMEL DIP

Makes 1¾ cups

Keep a bag of caramels in the pantry and a pound cake in the freezer and you'll be ready to serve Creamy Caramel Dip at your next impromptu gathering.

1 (14oz) bag KRAFT Caramels
⅔ cup half and half

1. Stir together caramels and half and half in a 4-cup glass measure.

STEP 2

3. Serve warm or at room temperature with fresh fruit, pound cake or angel food cake cubes.

STEP 1

2. Microwave on HIGH 4-5 minutes or until dip is smooth, stirring every minute.

STEP 3

Cook's Notes

⏱ TIME: Preparation takes 5 minutes. Cooking takes 5 minutes.

? VARIATION: Add 2 tbsps almond, coffee or Irish cream flavored liqueur. Decrease half and half to ½ cup.

◯ SERVING IDEA: Apples, pears, oranges and bananas are especially good fruits to serve with caramel dips.

CHOCOLATE CARAMEL PECAN CHEESECAKE

Serves 10-12

This recipe should definitely be added to your cheesecake repertoire. Expect rave reviews from all who taste it and be prepared to share the recipe with other cooks.

Crust

2 cups vanilla wafer crumbs
6 tbsps PARKAY Margarine, melted

Filling

1 (14oz) bag KRAFT Caramels
1 (5oz) can evaporated milk
1 cup chopped pecans
2 (8oz) packages PHILADELPHIA BRAND Cream Cheese, softened
½ cup sugar
2 eggs
1 cup BAKER'S Semi-Sweet Real Chocolate Chips, melted
1 tsp vanilla

STEP 3

4. In large mixing bowl, beat cream cheese and sugar at medium speed with electric mixer until well blended.

5. Add eggs, one at a time, mixing well after each addition. Blend in chocolate and vanilla; pour over pecans.

1. Preheat oven to 350°F.

2. Mix together crumbs and margarine. Press onto bottom and sides of 9-inch springform pan and bake for 10 minutes.

3. In small bowl, microwave caramels with milk on HIGH 4 to 5 minutes or until melted, stirring every minute. Pour over crust; top with pecans.

STEP 5

6. Place pan on cookie sheet. Bake 45 minutes. Loosen cake from rim of pan; cool before removing rim of pan. Chill several hours or overnight.

Cook's Notes

🕐 TIME: Preparation takes 35 minutes plus chilling. Baking takes 45 minutes.

🔪 PREPARATION: To soften cream cheese, microwave in bowl on MEDIUM (50%) 1 minute. To melt chocolate, microwave chocolate chips in small bowl on HIGH 1½-2 minutes or until almost melted, stirring after 1 minute. Stir until smooth.

📖 COOK'S TIP: The center of most cheesecakes should still appear soft when the cheesecake is removed from the oven, as it will firm as it cools.

CARAMEL PECAN PIE
Serves 8

This is a caramel version of the traditional favorite. Try it with peanuts, too.

½ (15oz) package refrigerated pie crust (1 crust)
36 KRAFT Caramels
¼ cup PARKAY Margarine
¼ cup water
½ cup sugar
3 eggs, beaten
½ tsp vanilla
1 cup pecan halves

1. Preheat oven to 350°F.

2. Prepare crust according to package directions for unbaked crust.

3. Melt caramels and margarine with water in heavy saucepan over low heat, stirring frequently until smooth.

STEP 3

4. Gradually add to combined sugar, eggs, vanilla and salt; mix well.

STEP 4

5. Stir in pecans and pour into pastry shell.

STEP 5

6. Bake 45 minutes. Filling will appear soft, but firms as it cools.

Cook's Notes

🕐 TIME: Preparation takes 15 minutes. Cooking takes 45 minutes.

❓ VARIATION: Substitute cashews, chopped walnuts or peanuts for pecan halves.

PRALINE SOUFFLE

Serves 6-8

Delight guests with a spectacular chilled caramel souffle. It's sprinkled with crunchy caramelized nuts and served with an orange liqueur-caramel sauce. Follow these step-by-step instructions carefully and you'll have a dessert to be proud of.

1 envelope unflavored gelatin
1½ cups cold water
28 KRAFT Caramels
2 tbsps sugar
3 egg yolks
3 cups whipping cream, whipped
2 tbsps sugar
¼ cup chopped pecans, toasted
1 cup KRAFT Caramel Topping
2 tbsps orange flavored liqueur

STEP 3

7. Melt 2 tablespoons sugar in skillet over medium heat until clear and caramel-colored. Stir in pecans.

8. Spoon onto greased cookie sheet and immediately separate pecans with two forks. Cool, then break into small pieces.

1. Soften gelatin in ½ cup water, stirring over low heat until dissolved.

2. Melt caramels and 2 tbsps sugar with remaining water over low heat, stirring until smooth.

3. Stir small amount of hot caramel mixture into egg yolks, then mix this into the remaining caramel mixture. Cook, stirring constantly, over low heat 3-5 minutes or until thickened.

4. Stir in gelatin. Chill until slightly thickened.

5. Fold caramel mixture into whipped cream.

6. Wrap 3 to 4-inch collar of foil around top of 1-quart souffle dish and secure with tape. Pour mixture into dish; chill until firm.

STEP 8

9. Stir together caramel topping and liqueur.

10. Remove foil collar and sprinkle pecans over souffle before serving. Serve with caramel sauce.

Cook's Notes

🕐 TIME: Preparation takes 40 minutes plus chilling.

🍞 COOK'S TIP: Be sure to use clean eggs free of cracks. Egg whites and yolks will separate most easily when at refrigerated temperature.

HEAVENLY HASH

Serves 8

This fluffy mixture of rice, fruit, marshmallows and nuts is an adaptation of a traditional Scandinavian dessert.

¼ cup slivered almonds
2 cups KRAFT Miniature Marshmallows
2 cups cooked MINUTE Rice, chilled
1 (8oz) can crushed pineapple, drained
½ cup maraschino cherry halves, drained
1 (8oz) container COOL WHIP Whipped Topping, thawed

1. Toast the almonds.

2. Combine marshmallows, rice, fruit and almonds.

3. Fold whipped topping into rice mixture. Chill.

STEP 3

STEP 2

Cook's Notes

⏱ TIME: Preparation takes 15 minutes plus chilling.

🍳 COOK'S TIP: To toast slivered almonds, place almonds in single layer in shallow baking pan. Bake at 350°F for 8 to 10 minutes or until golden brown.

◣ PREPARATION: Plan ahead for this dessert by making extra rice with an entrée the night before.

❓ VARIATIONS: Substitute one (20oz) can pineapple chunks, drained, for crushed pineapple. Increase cherries to ¾ cup.

SEAFOAM LIME MOLD
Serves 6

Choose an attractive mold for this creamy lime and pineapple gelatin salad.

1 (3oz) package JELL-O Lime Flavor Gelatin
1 cup boiling water
½ cup cold water
1 tbsp lemon juice
1 (8oz) package PHILADELPHIA BRAND Cream Cheese, softened
1½ cups KRAFT Miniature Marshmallows
2 (8oz) cans crushed pineapple, drained
½ cup chopped nuts
Lettuce and watercress

1. Dissolve gelatin in boiling water; add cold water and juice. Gradually add gelatin to cream cheese, mixing until blended.

2. Chill until thickened but not set, then fold in marshmallows, pineapple and nuts.

STEP 2

3. Pour into 6-cup ring mold, smooth, and chill until firm. Unmold onto serving plate and serve surrounded with lettuce and watercress.

STEP 1

STEP 3

Cook's Notes

⏱ TIME: Preparation takes 10 minutes plus chilling.

👨‍🍳 COOK'S TIP: When unmolding a gelatin salad, first use a small metal spatula or knife to loosen the edge of the gelatin from the mold. Dip the mold in warm water, up to the rim, for 10 to 15 seconds then shake the mold to loosen the gelatin. Moisten the serving plate so the gelatin can be repositioned after

unmolding, if necessary. Place the plate on top of the mold and invert, shaking to loosen gelatin.

◣ PREPARATION: Add the dissolved gelatin very gradually to the softened cream cheese to keep the mixture smooth and free of lumps.

CARAMEL BREAD PUDDING

Serves 6-8

This is a homey dessert with definite family appeal. Caramel sauce perfectly complements the cinnamon-spiced bread pudding.

36 KRAFT Caramels
¼ cup water
4 cups fresh bread cubes
3 eggs, beaten
2 cups milk
¼ cup sugar
1 tsp vanilla
½ tsp cinnamon

1. Preheat oven to 325°F.

2. Melt caramels with water over low heat, stirring until smooth. Place bread in greased 10 x 6-inch baking dish.

STEP 2

3. Combine remaining ingredients, pour over bread and top with caramel sauce.

STEP 3

STEP 3

4. Bake 55 minutes. Serve warm or cool.

Cook's Notes

 TIME: Preparation takes 20 minutes. Cooking takes 55 minutes.

SERVING IDEA: Served warm this dessert is the perfect winter warmer.

LUSCIOUS FREEZE PIE
Serves 6-8

If you have 10 minutes you have time to make a pie. This frozen pie is perfect for the summertime. Make it with your family's favorite flavor of sherbet – lime, orange or raspberry.

1 (8oz) package PHILADELPHIA BRAND Cream Cheese, softened
1 (7oz) jar KRAFT Marshmallow Creme
1 cup lime, orange or raspberry sherbet, softened
2 cups thawed COOL WHIP Whipped Topping
1 (9 inch) chocolate wafer crumb crust

1. Beat cream cheese and marshmallow creme at medium speed, with electric mixer, until well blended.

STEP 1

2. Add sherbet and mix well.

STEP 2

3. Fold in whipped topping, pour into crust and freeze until firm.

STEP 3

Cook's Notes

⏱ TIME: Preparation takes 10 minutes plus freezing.

❓ VARIATION: Use a graham cracker or vanilla wafer crumb crust for this pie.

⊙ SERVING IDEA: Serve garnished with whipped cream and lime slices, orange slices or raspberries, depending on the sherbet used.

DELICIOUS CARAMEL BROWNIES

Makes 2½ dozen

What a sweet-tooth satisfier – brownies with a caramel, chocolate and nut topping. A packaged brownie mix makes this recipe quick and easy.

---

1 (20-23oz) package brownie mix
1 (14oz) bag KRAFT Caramels
2 tbsps milk
1 cup mini semi-sweet chocolate chips
1 cup chopped nuts

---

1. Prepare and bake brownies according to package directions.

2. While brownies are baking, melt caramels with milk over low heat, stirring frequently.

3. Top hot brownies with caramel mixture and sprinkle with chocolate chips and nuts.

STEP 3

4. Cool slightly; chill. Cut into bars.

STEP 2

STEP 4

Cook's Notes

🕐 TIME: Preparation takes 15 minutes. Cooking takes 35 minutes.

❓ VARIATION: To microwave caramels, combine caramels and milk in 1½-quart bowl; microwave on HIGH 2½ to 3½ minutes or until smooth when stirred, stirring after each minute.

📖 COOK'S TIP: Store these brownies, covered, in the refrigerator.

CARAMEL CRISPY TREATS
Makes 3 dozen

Here's a caramel version of a favorite crispy rice cereal snack to take on your next picnic.

1 (14oz) bag KRAFT Caramels
2 tbsps PARKAY Margarine
2 tbsps water
8 cups crisp rice cereal

1. Microwave caramels, margarine and water in 1-quart glass bowl on HIGH 2½-3½ minutes or until smooth, stirring every minute. Alternatively, melt caramels with margarine and water over low heat in heavy saucepan, stirring until smooth.

2. Pour caramel mixture over cereal and toss until well coated.

STEP 2

3. Press into greased 13 x 9-inch baking pan. Let stand until firm. Cut into bars.

STEP 1

STEP 3

Cook's Notes

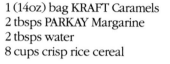 TIME: Preparation takes 15-20 minutes.

COOK'S TIP: Store Caramel Crispy Treats at room temperature.

PRACTICALLY FOOLPROOF MERINGUE

Covers one 9-inch pie.

Making meringue will never be intimidating again. With the secret ingredient – marshmallow creme – the meringue topping is very smooth, stable, and practically foolproof.

3 egg whites
Dash of salt
1 (7oz) jar KRAFT Marshmallow Creme

STEP 2

1. Preheat oven to 350°F.

2. Beat egg whites and salt until soft peaks form; gradually add marshmallow creme and beat until stiff peaks form.

3. Spread over pie filling, sealing to edge of crust.

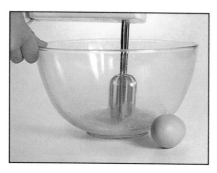

STEP 2

STEP 3

4. Bake 12-15 minutes or until lightly browned. Cool.

Cook's Notes

⏱ TIME: Preparation takes 10 minutes. Cooking takes 15 minutes.

🍞 COOK'S TIP: When spreading meringue on a pie be sure the meringue seals the crust all the way around, as this contact prevents the meringue from shrinking during baking.

🔪 PREPARATION: When cutting a pie topped with meringue use a wet knife.

THE ULTIMATE CHOCOLATE CARAMEL PECAN PIE

Serves 10-12

Pecan Pie may have originated in the South but now it's an all-American favorite. This version, with a pecan crust, caramel-pecan filling and chocolate topping, is fantastic!

Crust
2 cups pecans, finely chopped
¼ cup sugar
¼ cup PARKAY Margarine, melted

Filling
1 (14oz) bag KRAFT Caramels
¼ cup milk
1 cup pecans, chopped
8 (1oz) squares BAKER'S Semi-Sweet Chocolate
⅓ cup milk
¼ cup powdered sugar
½ tsp vanilla

1. Preheat oven to 350°F.

2. Combine pecans, sugar and margarine, mixing well. Press onto bottom and sides of 9-inch pie plate.

3. Bake for 12-15 minutes or until lightly browned. Cool.

4. Melt caramels with ¼ cup milk over low heat, stirring until smooth. Pour over crust.

5. Sprinkle pecans over melted caramels.

6. Melt chocolate with ⅓ cup milk and sugar over low heat, stirring until smooth. Stir in vanilla.

STEP 6

7. Pour over caramel nut filling, spreading chocolate mixture to edge of pie. Chill.

STEP 2

STEP 7

Cook's Notes

⏱ TIME: Preparation takes 35 minutes plus chilling.

◯ SERVING IDEA: Serve with sweetened whipped cream.

INDEX

Recipes developed by the Kraft Creative Kitchens
Photography by Peter Barry
Recipes prepared and styled by Helen Burdett
Designed by Judith Chant
Project co-ordination by Hanni Penrose